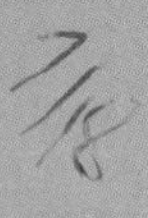

Emma Frost

BLOOM

Emma Frost
BLOOM

Writer: Karl Bollers
Pencilers: Carlo Pagulayan, Adriana Melo & Will Conrad
Inkers: Dennis Crisostomo, Will Conrad, Sean Parsons, Andrew Pepoy & Eric Cannon

Colorist: Transparency Digital
Letters: Virtual Calligraphy's Cory Petit & Dave Sharpe
Cover Art: Greg Horn
Assistant Editors: Stephanie Moore, Sean Ryan & Cory Sedlmeier
Editor: Mike Marts

Collection Editor: Jennifer Grünwald
Senior Editor, Special Projects: Jeff Youngquist
Director of Sales: David Gabriel
Production: Jerry Kalinowski
Book Designer: Carrie Beadle
Creative Director: Tom Marvelli

Editor in Chief: Joe Quesada
Publisher: Dan Buckley

PREVIOUSLY...

Young Emma turns her back on her father and the security of her wealthy Massachusetts home, choosing instead to seek her own fortune. Alone in Boston, Emma quickly befriends a dishwasher named Troy who is heavily indebted to local thugs. When Troy is unable to pay off the debt, the thugs kidnap Emma and hold her for ransom in a bid to extort a quarter of a million dollars from her father.

Emma uses her telepathic abilities to successfully heighten the distrust and paranoia within the minds of her kidnappers.They quickly turn against each other, allowing Emma to escape, but not before Troy loses his life.

Emma claims the ransom money as her own and relocates to New York City...

ISSUE 13

"Well, Emma, I must *truly* say..."
DEAN IRVINE
ACADEMIC ADVISOR

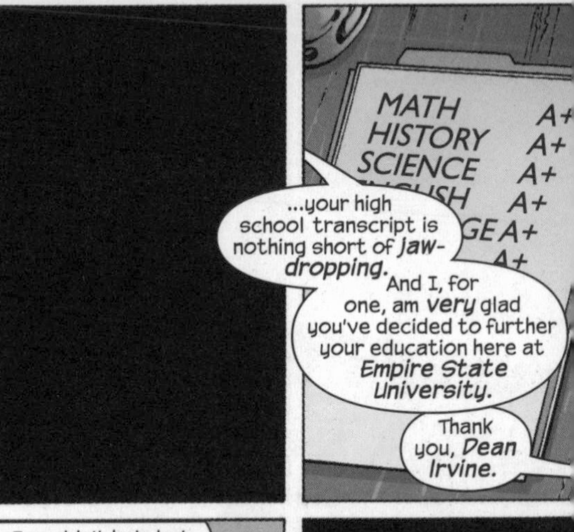
MATH A+
HISTORY A+
SCIENCE A+
...your high school transcript is nothing short of *jaw-dropping.*
And I, for one, am *very* glad you've decided to further your education here at *Empire State University.*
Thank you, *Dean Irvine.*

EMMA FROST
IN
BLOOM

I couldn't help but notice that you hail from one of Boston's *wealthiest* families.
Yes... my father's *paying* for my stay here.

Er, yes...uh, Emma, if you don't mind my asking...with such *outstanding* grades...
...and choices like Harvard...Yale... any school in the *nation,* really...

...what made you pick E.S.U.?

Guess I needed a *change.*

CHAPTER ONE: HARD KNOCKS
8 YEARS AGO...
Well, Emma, this is it. The start of a new life...
...attending college in New York City where no one knows you.
And if they did...
...they probably wouldn' recognize you.
Oh, God--I forgot to wear deodorant!
What's that funky odor?
...or suspect that you could read the minds.

Drop Famous Armenian Philosophers.
Add Intro to Media Studies.
Where the heck is the Natural Science building?

What the--?!
WHUMP

Oh, wonderful.

Sorry about that!
Heh...could anything more clichéd happen in an academic setting?

With you at the helm, who knows?
Here's a nugget for future reference--if you want to ask someone out on a date, don't pretend to accidentally bump into him--or her, in this instance--sending textbooks careening every which way.
It's rude.

And clichéd.

SOON...
Your father and I really think this room should be asbestos-proofed, chipmunk!
Mom! Dad! Will you, like, go to the airport already?! You're driving me--
Who's this?
How should I know? I just got here, Dad! Now, will you two please leave?
I'm Emma. I...think we're roommates.
Jack McDermott. This s my wife, Jill. Yeah, just like the nursery rhyme. It's a panic, ain't it?
I guess...
So, you're going to be sharing living quarters with our little chipmunk, hmm...?
Chip...?
ENOUGH!

SLAM
Christie McDermott.
Emma Frost.
So, we're roomies.
You like scente candles?

THE NEXT DAY
"Can any of you tell me what a 'balance sheet' is?
"Emma...?"
It's a statement that lists a company's assets, liabilities, and capital within a specific period of time.
Basically a "snapshot" of its financial standing.
Correct-- and very succinct, might add. Balance heets are commonly sed to determine a company's present value.
Now, can anyone give a definition of the term "accounts payable"?
Anyone besides Emma...?

Uhh... okay, then.
Emma...?
"Accounts payable" refers to the amounts owed by a company to outside suppliers of goods and services.
Why, ye--
And, in contrast, "accounts receivable" are amounts owed to a company by its customers for services rendered.
Uhh...right. I...I was going to...say that next...
Well, that's all the time we have for now. Don't forget to read the next four chapters by Thursday...
Hey, Emma!
Great. Now he knows my name.
I've got a question for you...

I know.
Well...?
Uhh...yeah. Heh...see, you told me how not to ask you out on a date the other day...
...but you never told me how to ask you out on a date, and I've been kinda wondering...
Look, Max, I--
Hey! You know my name!
s because I play on school basketball team, right? Fame t comes ith the rritory!
No. It's ecause I ppened to e paying ttention uring roll all in class today.
And because I'm psychic.
Well...that's cool, then. There's a big game tonight. Feel free to drop by and witness me making a fool out of myself! Hilarity will ensue! This I vow!
What a half-wit.

"So, like I was saying..."
...aging Hollywood actors dating women young enough to be their granddaughters. What's the word I'm looking for?
Gross? Putrid? Vomit-inducing?
Which brings me to my next question--like, who's supposed to actually believe these bean burritos are real?
So, you're majoring in education with a minor in business...? How many credits are you taking this semester?
Twenty-four.
Whoa! Planning on someday running a corporation like it's West Point?
Or maybe the other way around...
You g
girl!

How's life in the Fine Arts department?
Amazing! My parents always wanted me to be a doctor, but when I told them I wanted to be a sculptor...
...they were both really supportive.
st be... nice.
Emma...?
Are you okay?
Hm?
Oh, sorry... I just spaced for a sec. You were saying...?
Umm...I'm, like, taking four classes, twelve credits total, so loving the heck out of it, and my mentor...
...my mentor...
Sigh
You've got the hots for him.

Yes.
I mean, no!
Liar, liar.
No, it's just that...I think he's, like, really brilliant.
And sensitive.
And kinda cu--
Oh, yeah! He's going for it! He's going for it!
Then there's Max what's-his-face.
You want to talk about big men on campus, Emma? Max Devreaux is definitely one of 'em.
You're joking, right?
Not even a little!
I mean, is he a meathead? Check.
Does he know the difference between flat and silverware? Doubtful.
Has he ever listened to classi
music? Let's not
ourselves.
But those arms, Emma! Those pecs!
So, I should be glad he invited me to watch him play tonight?
He invited you to the game?! And you so said yes, right...?
I ignored hi
while walking a
in the opposit
direction.
Like. Wow.
Wow what?

Well, was he acting like a jerk when he asked you out?
He was checking out my butt.
Did he touch it?
Uh, no...
Cold.
You think I'm cold.
No, I never thought that.
Yes, you did.
No, I didn't.
Again with the lying.
Okay, maybe I thought it.
It's just that I don't understand why an attractive coed with no boyfriend would blow off a handsome-enough varsity basketball player.
KRASH
Why indeed?

THAT NIGHT...
30
ESU
ESU

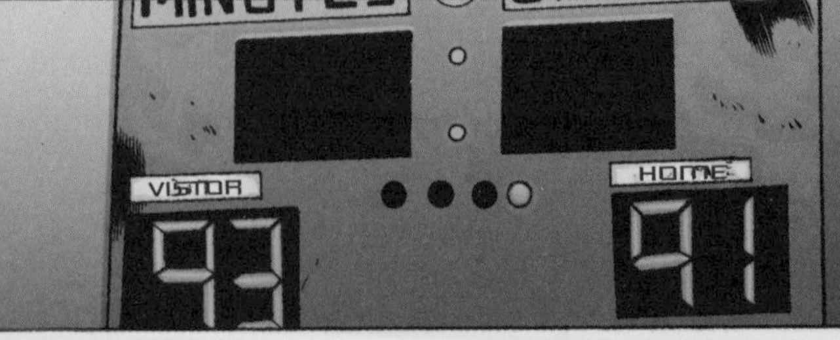
VISITOR
HOME
93
91

Emma, did you see that? Max just waved to you!
He was waving to the *stands,* Christie.

Honestly, Emma...how can you be so nonplussed when there's less than two minutes left to the game and the home team is down by 2 points?
Guess I'm just not a *sports fan...*

E-Emma...?

HOME
94
3

Emma...?
What *happened* back there?

I... I don't *know.*

"Frost...?"
Has anyone seen Emma Frost?
Remember, folks, three or more unexcused absences will reflect negatively on your final grade.
LATER...
Why did my powers go haywire at the game? Felt like someone kicked me in the forehead.
Haven't experienced pain like that since the beginning.
How the heck did I get these weirdo abilities, anyway?
I was so bent on keeping them a secret, I never really stopped to question where they came from. Now, I might be losing control of them and if I don't get it back...
...I may be forced to leave school an go somewhere far from people.

Hey! Hey! Hey!

eesh! Can we, e, have a *little* bit of light in here?
Sure.
Anyways, look what I brung ya. Vittles! Chow! Grub!

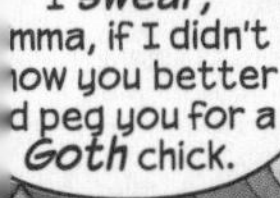
I *swear,* mma, if I didn't ow you better d peg you for a *Goth* chick.

We've got all the essential food groups. Chicken "butt"let parmigiana. Ramen impersonating angel hair. Your basic garden salad, and last but not *least...*
Dessert?

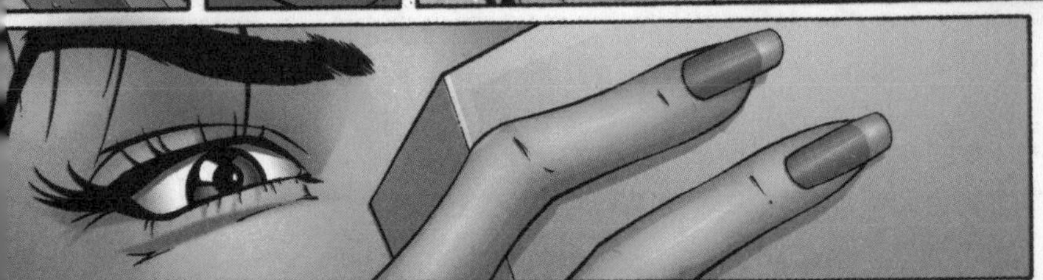

Froot Hoops!

Oh, no.
She's finally worked up the *nerve.*

Yo, roomie, while bringing you meals every day for the past week has fostered my more *maternal* side...
...which I don't know that I'm all that *comfortable* with...
...all joking aside, you haven't left the dorms in a *week.* Not since the so-called "incident," and I'm worried about you.
I'll be *fine,* Christie.
Not if you keep missing classes and eventually flunk out of school you *won't...*
What's got you so freaked?
Max asked about you today...
What did *he* want?
He wanted to know where on earth--
KNOCK KNOCK
Oh, man--he's *early!*
Sure.
Listen, Emma, can we discuss this later? I've kinda sorta gotta be someplace with my *mentor.*
Hello, Christie, how are you?
Just great, Ian, come on--
Ian

M-my old teacher!
--in?

ISSUE 14

MPIRE STATE UNIVERSITY
Emma?
Ian!
You're Christie's roommate? And...and blonde?
Contacts.
Uhh... bleached. And you're her mentor? And...and you look... different.
Hold up-- you guys know each other?!
Ooh, boy.
"MUTIE" BLOOM
PART 2 of 6

It's a...long story.
I was Emma's high school art teacher.
Man! What are the odds of you two running into each other after all this time? Talk about kismet!
Shoot me now.
It's really good to see you, Emma.
Really?
You too, Ian.
Well, I was just about to do the wash, and lord knows it won't do itself--
--so why don't I just leave you and Christie to whatever it is you're--
Step away from the laundry basket, miss!
Christie...!
You have five seconds to comply.
Seriously, roomie, I'll put the laundry in the wash while you and Ian take a few minutes to catch up.
Oh no.
See ya in a few!

She went and left.
Emma...? You okay?
N-never better.
So...you and Christie have a really nice dorm room here.
Back when I was in college, my roommate and I didn't have half as much style...
...but I guess that comes from being a couple of guys. And slobs.
I-I had no right to kiss you, Ian.
W-what did she just say?
I said I had no right to kiss you.
In Boston.
In the car.
Oh.
That's what I thought she said.
I...I remember... but come on, Emma...

...every schoolgirl should be allowed at least one crush. Right?
So you don't blame me?
Because that kiss cost me my job at Snow Valley? Of course not.
Your father simply misinterpreted what he saw before getting all the facts.
He does that sometimes.
On purpose.
Believe me, I'm a lot happier being an academic advisor and mentor here at E.S.U. In a way...
...that kiss set me free.
Hi, honey! I'm home!
Hey, Emma-- Ian and I are going to a gallery opening in Soho tonight. Want to come with?
I...think I'll pass if that's okay.
Emma's a recluse, Ian. She doesn't go anywhere. Not even to class!

Ooops!
Emma, is this true?
You've been skipping classes? Is your father somehow responsible?
No! I-It's nothing, Ian. Really.
It doesn't sound like nothing to me.
This isn't like you at all. You were my star pupil in high school, Emma.
Why don't you stop by my office early next week so we can talk it over?
A-all right.
But in the meantime, promise me you'll go to class?
O-okay... I promise.

THE NEXT DAY...
MUTANTS MENACE TO MANKIND
PROTECT US HUMANS
THEY'RE AMONG US
TEST ATHLETE 4 MUTATION!
TEST ATHLETES FOR MUTATION!
MUTANTS ARE HAZARDS
Yeah. Haven't you been reading the newspapers? Or watching the *news?*
No, not really.
These mutants... scientists are saying that they're supposed to be this *new breed* of human.
The next rung on the evolutionary ladder. They've been popping up for the last *year* or so.

MUTIES MEAN
PRO HUMAN
MUTANTS THREAT
LAY BY THE RULES
MUTANT = CHEATERS
What...?
SIGN UP
A student *protest?*
RADIOACTIVE LIARS
UMANS RULE
I'M A MUTANT
AGENTS of DESTRUCTION GENETIC TERRORISTS
But the signs hey're carrying ake absolutely *no sense.*
Good to see ou again, Emma. n't mind *them...* ey've been at it all morning.
Hey, Max. So...I don't get it. What the heck are they supposed to be *protesting?*
Haven't you heard? Some star athlete in California was revealed to be a mutant.
A... *mutant?*
But what makes them *different* from the rest of us?
They're born ith these strange, r lack of a better word, *"super-powers".*
It makes 'em able to do things *we can't* like fly through the air without wires, walk straight through solid walls...
...and read people's *minds.*

WHUMP!
Emma? You okay?
Uhh... sure, Max, it's just that... well, it all sounds pretty scary, y'know?
Totally. Though you can't blame me for dropping your books this time, huh?
LIONS BUIL
I guess not...
I can't stand those stinking muties!
They're a bunch of no-good freaks. That's what they are.
Their thoughts-- so filled with hatred.
If it were legal, I'd kill every last one of 'em.
They think they're superior to us, but they're wrong!
I wish they'd all just die so the world could go back to normal.
What if I'm a mutant, too?
Hey, Emma-- where you going?
Sorry, Max, but I've got to run or I'll be late for class!
But wait! I wanted to ask you...
...something.
YA AIN'T
AGENT

LATER...
I'm shaking like a leaf.
If I'm really one of these mutant people...
...what would happen to me if the rest of the world found out? They'd know I used my powers to pass my exams.
Emma...?
Uh-oh!
Can you tell me which early home-schooling pioneer I'm referring to?
Uhh...
John Holt.
...John Holt...?
Hunh. For a moment there I thought you weren't paying attention.
Okay, does anyone have a question?
Kai...?
Should mutants be allowed to go to school with...you know...normal kids?
DUKE

Well, why shouldn't they, Kai?
Just because mutants are different doesn't mean they should be denied the same basic rights as everyone else.
Everyone deserves an education.
Who says? Everything I've seen on TV says that mutants are a dangerous threat.
Do you believe everything you see o TV, Shannon?
When it comes to mutants? Definitely. Could you imagine some mutant bully on the playground vaporizing defenseless students for their milk money?
Not really, Shannon. No.
And if that situation were to ever happen, the kid's problem would be that he's a sociopath, not a mutant.

What do you think, Professor Mason? Should mutants be allowed to attend school with "normal" children?
Not if I have anything to say about it.
I refuse to have this discussion in my classroom, Emma, and that's all I'm going to say on the matter.
I read you loud and clear.

OON...
Emma! Em-maaa!
Hey, Christie. Why so excited?
Well...I just spoke with Max Devreaux in Spanish 100.
My condolences.
Seriously, Emma. What has that poor guy ever done to you?
Nothing, really...besides annoy me.
Yeah, but it's only because he likes you and wants to get to know you better.
Don't tell me you're one of thos weirdos...
W-what kind of weirdo?!
The kind that hates some-body just for liking them. That'd be more twisted than a pretzel at the chiro-practor's!
So prove to me you're not a pretzel with bac pains and come with me to the party Max and his teammates are throwing tonight.
He invited us both.
Okay, Christie. You're on.

So what do you think?
Emma, you look *fabulous!*
Which color should I wear?
I'd go with *white.*
Yes, ma'am!
She's in a
awfully goo
mood.
I can tell she has a crush on *Ian,* eve
if she won't *admit* it
And they did atten
that gallery openin
last night.
Is she...is sh
involved wi
him?
I could just *ask* her flat-out...
...then read her thoughts to know whether she's telling the *truth* or not.
But it's none of my business. I have *no right* to pry in someone else's private affairs...
...or *do* I?
If I'm *really* one
these mutants Ma
was describing...

...then wouldn't I just be using my *innate talent?*
What's wrong with *that?*

So, Christie, how'd it go last night?
Last *night...?*
With you and Ian...? You know, at the gallery opening...?

Oh.
It was... cool.
He's amazing.

Amazing?! What does she *mean* by that?
Just cool?
I had the best time of my life.
Yeah... you know how *stuffy* the Soho set can be.

Clik
She has this *huge* crush on him, yet she's trying to act like she *doesn't.*
Uhhh, actually, I'm from *Boston...*
Why?

LATER...
Hi, Max!
Whu--? I don't believe it!
Emma Frost and Christie McDermott? This is just too crazy for words! I might die from shock!
I'm dying. Can't you tell?
That's real, uhh... great, Max.
Here--why don't I take your jackets so you two can get comfortable?
Thanks!
I thought I'd hate being here, but it's actually kind of nice...
E.S.U.
...and my powers seem to be under control again.
See, Emma? I told you this wouldn't hurt!
What can I say, Christie? You were right!

d there's Max. His thoughts like an open book. Feels like reading somebody's diary.
Come on. You can do it.
st ask her if she wants dance. It's no biggie, man. u're a varsity basketball yer.
Poor thing. He could use some help.
Say, Emma...I... uhh...
Want to dance?
Uh-- sure!
Arrivederci, guys!
Bon voyage!
Uh, Max...
...why aren't you dancing?
Well, the thing of it is...
...I really don't know how to dance.
You don't know how to...? Then why bother asking me?

Um--I didn't ask you, you asked me!
-sigh-

Out of our way, punk!
CRASH
Hey! What happened to the tunes?

Who the--?
Oh, no.
The basketball players from the school that lost last week's game to E.S.U.
So what brings you jokers here? Interested in seeing how winners party?

ot quite. You see, er we watched that report about that utie who secretly sed his powers to win at sports...
...me and the guys got to thinking.
And what? You managed to come up with a brain cell? What are you getting at?
...it doesn't make sense.
Our team hadn't lost a game this entire season, and suddenly we go up against you guys and... and...
Maybe he's the mutant. With the ability to ignore reality!
What'd you say, wise guy?
Breath mint. Would it kill you?
I knew I should have stayed in tonight.

Christie, we've got to get help!
How are we supposed to do that, Emma? The door's blocked!
I've got to do something before someone gets seriously hurt.
But what?
I can barely use my powers to control one of them, much less all.
Well, if I can't stop the fighting that way, I'll have to find another.
Maybe if I try to reach out with my mind...
...I can...
...call for...

Help.
Frank?! What'd you say?
We have to get to the on-campus apartments. Now!
Look out!

All right, boys and girls...

...break it up!

MINUTES LATER...
They're taking in anyone who was fighting.
Including Max. I hope he's not in trouble.
Isn't it weird the way the campus police just showed up like that, Emma?
Maybe they got an anonymous tip.
Can you believe thos losers? Crashing the party just to accuse Max and the basketba team of being mutants?
It's insane!
Everybody knows that mutants are disgusting freaks of nature who shoot laser-beams from their butts!
Max is way too cute for that, wouldn't you agree?
Oh... absolutely.

THE NEXT DAY...
I don't understand. Do everyday people generally *hate* mutants?
Even *regular* people, like Christie, who are otherwise nice?

The entire situation disturbs me... especially since I'm not sure which category I fit into.
I wish there was *someone* I could talk to...*confide* in...

Wait a minute.
There *is* someone.

EMPIRE STATE UNIVERSITY
VISUAL ARTS BUILDING
Ian...

...but...he's not *alone*...
...he's with *Christie!*

I should have *known.*

Men.
They're not worth it.
Wha--?

Trust me.
W-Who are you?
Bloom, darling. Name's Astrid Bloom.

ISSUE 15

EMPIRE STATE UNIVERSITY
Well?
Aren't you going to say something?
I--I can hear you in my *head.* How can that *be?*
"MUTIE" BLOOM
PART 3 of 6

I'm projecting my thoughts, darling.
My voice. And yet I don't feel the need to move my lips whatsoever.
Then-- then--that means you're a--a--
A mutant? You bet.
Why?

Aren't you?
Are-- are you kidding me? N-no way!
No? Isn't that the reason you came here to see Ian Kendall, your old high school teacher upon whom you had the crush to end all crushes?
All of the on-campus, anti-mutant hysteria that's been going on had you scared silly.
You felt he was the only person you could trust to tell your secret.
There's no point in lying to someone who can read thoughts.

What do you want from me?
What do I want?

...I want to be friends.

Do you know what it's been like for me? I thought I was the only one with abilities remotely like these.

Then boom! I suddenly discover there's someone else like me going to university right here in New York City. It's exciting!

How did you find me?

Actually, it was more like ou found me. I kept hearing ur mind crying out over and ver. It was all I could do to op myself from going batty!

I'm sorry... n...what's your name again?

First name: Astrid. Last name: Bloom.

I'm Emma. Emma Frost.

So, Astrid, does anyone know why it happens? Why mutants are born with these weird...gifts?
They say it's evolution...
...but, if you want my humble opinion, no one really knows why, Emma. It just is.
And the ones like us, who can read minds, they're called "telepaths"?
That's what they also say.
Though it's a bit more than just reading minds, if you want my humble opinion once more.
How do you know so much about all of this?
Read a few texts on the subject by this chap named Xavier. That, and some articles in Scientific American.
I don't get it...how could you not take full advantage of that vast library in your parents' mansion?
You read my thoughts like they're laid out on cue cards or something.

I wonder if--
NO!
I--I can't read her thoughts! Does--does she know I just tried?
Is she reading my mind right now?
MUTIES LEAVE!
What on--?
MUTIES LEAVE!
KEEP IT PURE!
DOWN WITH DARWIN!
MUTIES LEAVE!
DOWN WITH DARWIN!
Where on earth do they want us to go? Ugh. The Neanderthals.

MUTIES LEAVE!
DOWN WITH DARWIN!
Why do they *hate* us so much, Astrid?
Who doesn't envy birds their wings?
That's interesting...your *inner* voice doesn't sound the same as your *speaking* voice.
Oh, really? How does my inner voice sound?

It reminds me of a Bach concerto.
Then I'll be sure to use that voice--my real voice--whenever you and I communicate, Emma.
MUTIES LEAVE!
HUMANITY NOW!

MUTIES LEAVE! MUTIES LEAVE!
Want to grab some dinner?
Like *crazy.* I'm famished!

LATER...
Astrid...
...when you said dinner I didn't think you meant "actual" dinner!
I can't fathom how you've managed dining on campus fare this long, Emma.
Why spend all of your time there...
...when there's an entire world to be seen?
Budweiser
COKE
NIKE
WILL CONRAD
JVC

Take Bill for instance. Third generation New York City police officer.
His father was a detective. His brother is a detective. But Bill's a traffic cop.
The truth of the matter is Bill doesn't want to be a traffic cop. He doesn't want to be a detective, either.
He wants to climb Everest. But someone told him a long time ago that such a thing wasn't possible and he made the mistake of believing them.
Meet Janice. Homeless going on fifteen years. Doesn't speak a word of English.
Her late husband was a furrier who owned his own store on 30th Street.
When he died, she just sort of...gave up. She's actually got four mink stoles in her pushcart.

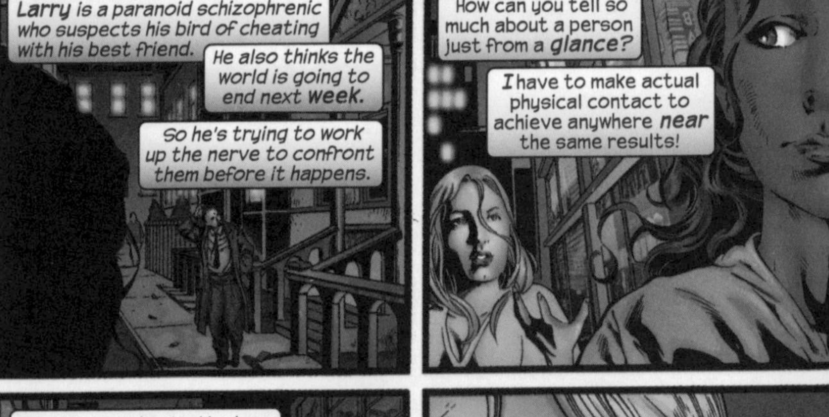
Larry is a paranoid schizophrenic who suspects his bird of cheating with his best friend.
He also thinks the world is going to end next week.
So he's trying to work up the nerve to confront them before it happens.
How can you tell so much about a person just from a glance?
I have to make actual physical contact to achieve anywhere near the same results!

Frankly, I'm shocked by how limited you are in the use of your mutant abilities, Emma. You've been in possession of them since high school...
...yet you can only read surface thoughts and just barely cast illusions.
Well...I don't think it's right to casually delve into a person's life history that way.

Oh? So, it's only okay to read minds to **cheat** on one's exams? Is that how the song goes, darling?
treet
Haven't *you* ever done the same?
No.
Well...technically, it's **not** really cheating since I'm not spying on anybody's exam papers...and anyway...
...pillaging a person's most intimate memories is **worse** than casually skimming their minds for some stupid test answers.
ow, you're simply **rationalizing** n order to justify your actions. I use my abilities so I can better xperience the human condition.
ho knows? Maybe it will help e be a better psychologist once I earn my master's degree. Tell me...
...what do you gain from using your powers **besides** good grades?
It's totally **unfair** of you to judge me like that, Astrid. I mean, what do **I** know about **you?** When I try to read **your** mind all I see is a **brick wall!**
CAFE
BROADWAY
Of **course** you do. That's because I've learned how to **shield** my thoughts.

I...I don't understand how you became so skilled at using your powers.
Then I'll have to show you...
...won't I?
UNDERGROUND
When I was no older than seven years of age ...
...my old man died from coronary failure.
Mum and I were basically left to fend for ourselves, but she made me a promise.
Mummy will always love you, Astrid, no matter what.
Eleven months after Dad kicked, she met Aubrey Chilton. It didn't take long for the two to tie the knot.
I missed my father, but found it within myself to be happy for Mum. For both of them.

It wasn't long after there came another arrival to our home...
...when Mum and step-dad returned from hospital with my newborn baby sister. Yvonne.
The change happened almost immediately. They converted my bedroom into a nursery for her...
...and I was made to sleep on the living room couch.
As the months dragged on, Mum's attitude toward me shifted drastically, but I truly believed that somewhere, deep down inside, she still loved me.
Then one day...
Yes, my darling. mmy loves you est, doesn't she now?
I'd been tossed out of my mother's heart. I didn't need telepathic abilities to know that...
...but four years later...
...at age thirteen...

...I got them anyway.
I made the mistake of confiding in my so-called family. They rejected me utterly. So I ran away from home.
Uhnnn...
Steady now.
Ever since that day, I've had to become adept in the use of my extra talents just to make it out here on my own.
I...I want to d
everything yo
can, Astrid.
Will you teach me
Absobloodylutel
darling.

U. CAMPUS--1 A.M.
What a *day!*
I still can't believe it happened.
I never *imagined* I'd find someone who can do the same things I can. But Astrid somehow does.
With *style.*
I wonder where *Christie* is? She's usually...home...
..by...now...
ZZZZZZZZZ
8 A.M.
Yawwwnn
Huh.

9 A.M.
Hey, Astrid.

Good morning, Emma.
I hope you got enough sleep to mentally prepare you for today's regimen.
I--

Hey, Emma!
Hi, Max!

What's going on?
Uhh... not a whole lot.
Who's the babe magnet, darling?
Um, Max...this is Astrid.

Hey.
Hey.
Say, have we met before? You look familiar.
Ever been to London?
No, it wasn't there...

So, Max, what happened the other night? I mean, players from a rival basketball team crashed your party, accused you of being a mutant, and a fight broke out between both teams!
What happened after campus public safety showed up?
Well, they hauled us off...
...then grilled us one by one about how the fight began... that jerk captain of the other team says I started it.
But it was his team that snuck onto campus!
Yeah, but I shoved him first.
So, they sent me to the dean of admissions. She threatened to take away my scholarship...
...and said I'd be expelled from E.S.U. if anything like it happens again.
You are aware that it was you he was trying to impress by going all medieval at the party.
What are you--?
You've found quite a gallant one here, luv. You should really give him a fairer shake.
you kindly
op reading
my mind?
And his?
So then the President of Burma steps in and says to the alien leprechaun in my gym locker, "This is nothing like the rigatoni Aunt Brenda used to make!"
Uhhh... sorry, Max. I didn't mean to zone out.

I've, uh, got a *lot* on my mind.
That's okay, Emma.

Just remember that I can lend an ear...
To perhaps *nibble* on.
...if you ever need somebody to talk to, Emma.
Your friend--she doesn't do much in the way of *talking,* huh? Shy type?
Something along those lines...

I'll catch you later, Emma! Nice meeting you, Astrid!

Will you do me a *huge* favor?

Stop reading your mind? Done deal, darling.

1 A.M.
What are we doing all the way up here?
Gaining a vantage.

Wow. Cool.

One could go so far as to say.
Down there is a sea of bubbling psyches. Sifting through each requires painstaking focus to enable one to deafen out the others and access the thoughts of a single individual. It's difficult...

...but not impossible.

Ooh!

There's Dean Irvine! My academic advisor. I want to try him first.
Okay, but concentrate...

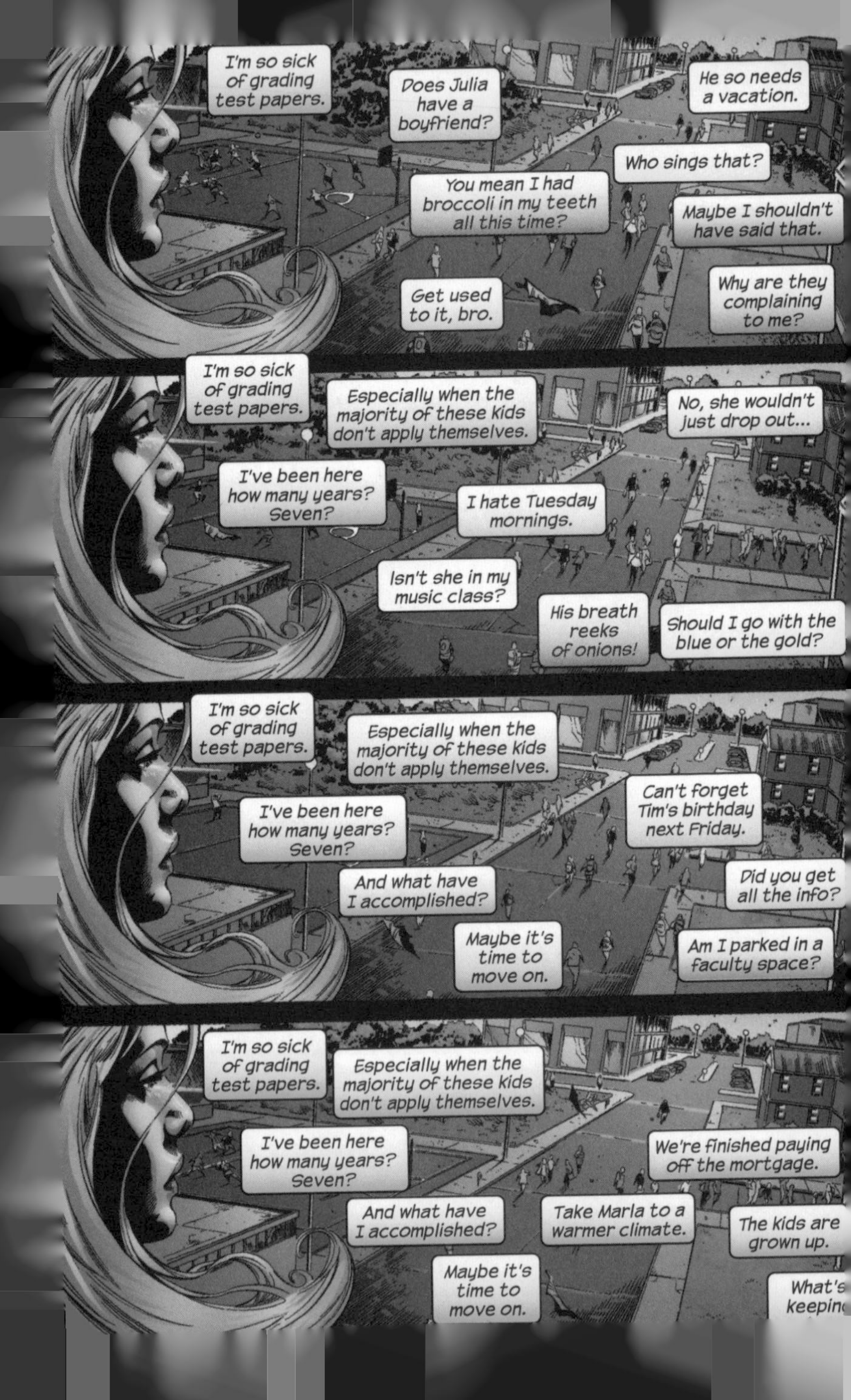

I'm so sick of grading test papers.
Does Julia have a boyfriend?
He so needs a vacation.
Who sings that?
You mean I had broccoli in my teeth all this time?
Maybe I shouldn't have said that.
Get used to it, bro.
Why are they complaining to me?
I'm so sick of grading test papers.
Especially when the majority of these kids don't apply themselves.
No, she wouldn't just drop out...
I've been here how many years? Seven?
I hate Tuesday mornings.
Isn't she in my music class?
His breath reeks of onions!
Should I go with the blue or the gold?
I'm so sick of grading test papers.
Especially when the majority of these kids don't apply themselves.
Can't forget Tim's birthday next Friday.
I've been here how many years? Seven?
And what have I accomplished?
Did you get all the info?
Maybe it's time to move on.
Am I parked in a faculty space?
I'm so sick of grading test papers.
Especially when the majority of these kids don't apply themselves.
I've been here how many years? Seven?
We're finished paying off the mortgage.
And what have I accomplished?
Take Marla to a warmer climate.
The kids are grown up.
Maybe it's time to move on.

Oh, my goodness. Dean Irvine's going to retire...
Forget Irvine and his lame drama, Emma.
How did it feel?
It wasn't as difficult as I thought it would be. The closest thing I can compare it to would be...
...tuning a radio to just the right station.
Now, don't you know infinitely more about the fellow than you would have with all that other noise buzzing about?
It was way more than I ever needed to know about the poor guy, but I have to admit...
...it was incredibly easy!
Let's not award ourselves a gold star just yet...
...we still have to teach you to tap into a person's memories without getting all touchy-feely...

7 P.M.
Boy.
Am.
I.
Bushed.
Feels like I'm receiving a second education from Astrid in addition to the one I'm already getting here.
But right *now*, the only thing I *feel* like getting is some--
Hey, Emma! Like, *where* have you been all day?
Where have *I* been? I was worried *sick* when you didn't come home last night, Christie.
Where have *you* been?
Where have I been?

Oh... nowhere.
I was with the most wonderful man in the world.
Ian?!

ISSUE 16

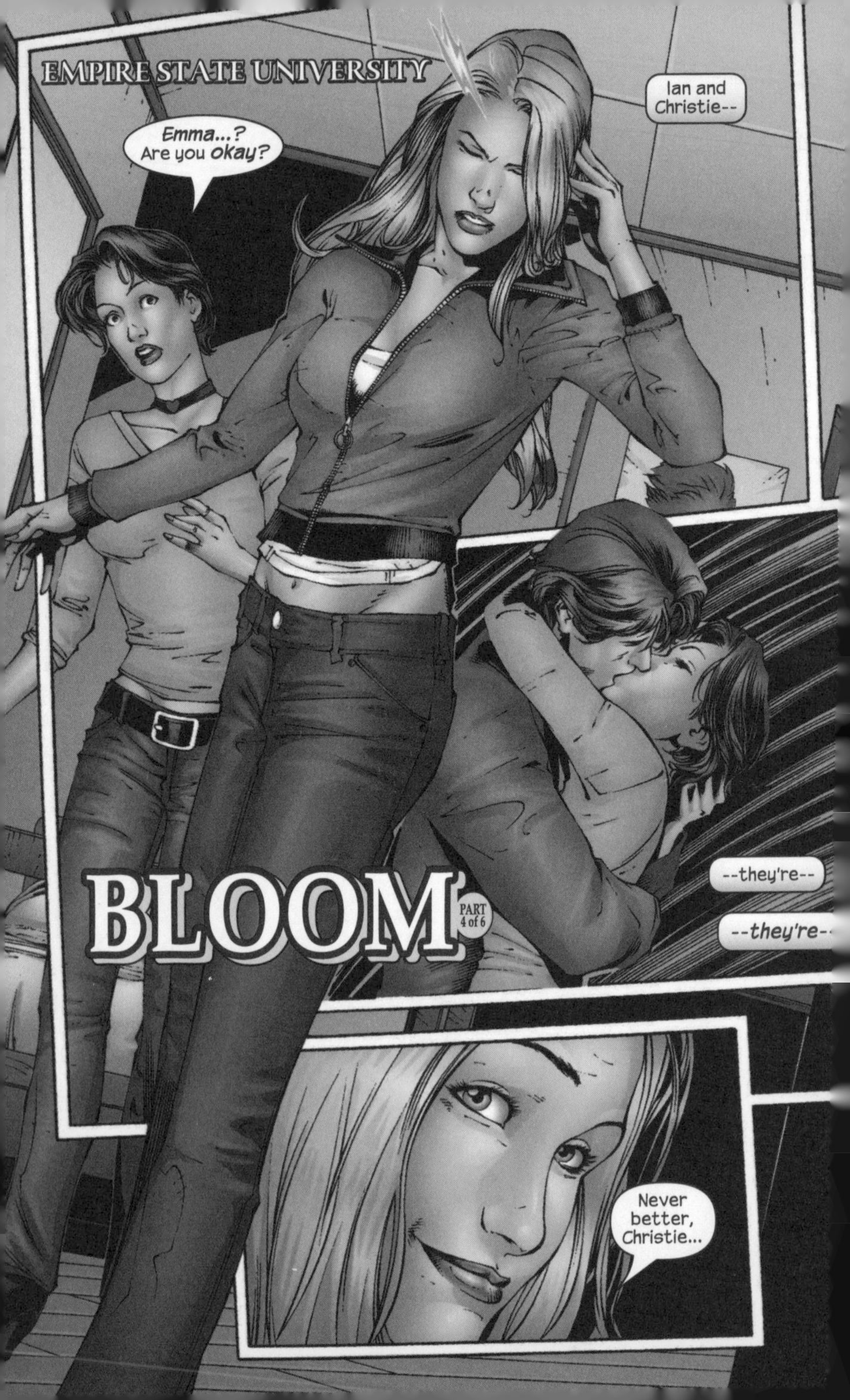

EMPIRE STATE UNIVERSITY
Emma...? Are you *okay*?
Ian and Christie--
BLOOM
PART 4 of 6
--they're--
--*they're*--
Never better, Christie...

feel like you're hiding something from me.
Hiding something...?
come home last night and your only response to where you've been is, "Nowhere."
If I didn't know any better, I'd think you found some romance.
Hey, roomie, I'm sorry...
"...but my parents flew in from Wisconsin yesterday to pay me a surprise visit.
"They insisted on taking me out for a night on the town...
"...and since I didn't have any class today, I said, 'What the hey, why not make them happy for once?'
6th Avenue
"And as the evening wore on..."

"...I was just too pooped to make it back to campus...
"...so I crashed at the hotel where they were staying."
Sorry I didn't call to let you know I wasn't butchered by a axe murderer, Emma.
Well, I'm just glad you're okay...
...you liar!
Your folks didn't pay you any "surprise visit" yesterday...
...and if they did, the only place you'd want to go is to the airport to get them on the next available flight home!
Anywho, I have to get a book from the library before it closes. Wanna come with?
I'll pass.
Okay, see ya later!
See you...
Traitor.

And?

How is this at all relevant to our lives, darling?
It's relevant, Astrid, because I wanted to show you what a conniving strumpet my roommate has turned out to be...

Well what did you expect, Emma? She's only human. Now...
...can we get on with today's game plan?
I guess. What's the lesson?
The rudiments of mind-control. Observe.

Professor Pinter brings his pet canine Elvis to campus with him each Wednesday. He routinely follows up his mid-morning lecture with pickled salmon on pumpernickel.
After which, he takes Elvis for a post-lunch stroll.

And every time, like clockwork...
Elvis!
...Elvis breaks away from the Professor and races off...

...to terrorize the pigeons.
But, today...
...they're not going without a fight!
What on--?!
Run, Elvis! Run!
Teach me how to do that so I can introduce Christie to heavy traffic.

Emma, that's sick! Taking control of an animal's mind is one thing, but doing it to another human being-- it's completely unethical--
--and should only be resorted to in a life or death situation!

Okay, Astrid. Relax! Seriously. I was just kidding.
It's in no way, shape, or form, funny.
Well, excuse me for not being ecstatic about my so-called roommate locking lips with my first big crush and not being brave enough to tell me!

It's none of your bloody business, Emma!
Besides, if you came to university to earn a degree, shouldn't you be focusing more on your schooling and less on some bird's love life?

You've more important matters to attend to, anyway...
...one of them being how to pass exams without rummaging through the thoughts of your poor, unwitting classmates.

H-how do you expect me to do that?

Oh, I don't know...

EMPIRE STATE UNIVERSITY LIBRARY
your deepest issue in every confusion
AGGHH!
the more perfect a thing is
he's all quitter, Rocky
Venus, I am yours
tomorrow and tomorrow and tomorrow
T-Too m-many thoughts--
--buzzing all around!
Don't freak out, Emma. Instead, concentrate.
Uhnnn...
Visualize a means of keeping them out. Visualize something strong.

...by studying, perhaps?
Shhh...
Steady there, luv.
Ladies, I'm going to have to ask you both to leave if you can't find a way to control yourselves.

Everything's under control.
Okay...what just happened exactly?
When human minds are engaged in reading and studying, their thoughts are less guarded, yet incredibly more organized.
Highly susceptible to telepathic reception.
I received my entire secondary education hanging out in public libraries and attending free seminars where I'd "piggyback" other people's thoughts.
That way, I didn't just acquire my own knowledge...
...I acquired everybody else's, too.
PLS OBSERVE
BULLETIN BOARD
Wow. I'm impressed.
It's beyond impressive, darli
Now come...
...you've got tons more to learn!

WO DAYS LATER...
I think that Maria Montessori's emphasis on self-determination and self-realization as part of the child's curriculum is the *linchpin* of true learning, Doctor Genn.

I'm very *impressed* with your knowledge of the early pioneers of education, Emma.

Why, thank y--
Quit showing off.

I'll see you Thursday, Doctor.
Take care, Emma.

Hey, Astrid.
NAILBOMB
Auditioning for the role of "Little Miss Brown-nose"?
Shut up!

Here comes your friend. The basketball star.
Max.
Oh, Emma, he's going to ask you out!
Astrid, you're right!
Funny thing is, I actually feel bad about having to say no.
I wonder how I can break it to him gentl without hurting his feelings.
Why do you have to break it to him at all? Why not give Max a test run? He certainly seems like a nice enough one.
Now you sound like my roommate.
Hmm...could be...
...or could be you're afraid of going out with the fellow.
Afraid? And wha pray tell, do I ha to be afraid of

That you'll start liking him and stop liking Ian.
This is all about you wanting to hit the rewind button and have things go back to the way they were in high school...
...but life isn't like that, luv. It's about transition. A changing of the guard.
wanted ad
I'd better give you two some privacy...
Hey, Emma!
Hi, Max! I'd love to go to the movies tomorrow night!
Uh, yeah...okay, cool.

THE FOLLOWING EVENING...

This is really *awesome,* Emma!
I'm so glad you finally saw the light and decided to give *Max* a shot.
Anything to distract me from you and Ian, eh?
Yeah... where *was* my head?

So, Christie... what have you been up to these last few days?
Oh, you know...it's been nothing but--

"--work--

"--work--

"--and *more* work."

Well, be sure not to *kill* yourself...

...unless it's excruciatingly *painful.*

THAT NIGHT...

HEAVENLY CREATURES
Whoa.
What's the matter, Max?
I had no idea that movie was going to be so *twisted.* It blew my mind. Not exactly a *date movie,* huh?

I think it's *good* to have your mind blown every now and again.
It's going to give me *nightmares!*
I didn't think you were the type to get bothered by nightmares, Max.
Quick--let's change the subject.

You like *pizza?*

PIZZA

So tell me, Max...
...are you or are you not a mutant?
Who needs to be a mutant, Emma? Scouts from the NBA are going to be lining up to sign me come graduation.
Would blue fur really be a plus?
Anyway, if I were a mutant, I wouldn't try to pass myself off as a regular human so I could get a leg up on the next guy. That's like an eighth-grader pretending to be in pre-school. Where's the challenge?
LATER...
Now, was that so bad?
I have to admit, as far as dates go, it wasn't half-bad...
So, you had a...good time?
Yes, a really good time.
Cool.

He wants to kiss me goodnight.
Of course he wants to kiss me goodnight.
Do I want him to kiss me goodnight?
I don't know if I'm ready to be kissed goodnight.

Max.
Emma...
Listen, I'm not sure where we're headed, but wherever it is, I'd like us to take our time getting there.

Here comes the speech I've been so looking forward to!
What?

And why am I not the least bit surprised?
Max... what did I say...?
What didn't you? You've acted like some kind of superior being from day one, Emma!

What are you talking about? None of that is true!
Sure it is! Admit it. You thought I was some brainless jock who was too stupid to have a meaningful conversation!

Admit it!
UFF!

Hey! That didn't tickle, Max!
"That didn't tickle, Max!"
This isn't funny.

"This isn't funny."
D-don't come any closer-- I'm warning you.
During freshman orientation they told all the students--

--if we ever got into a situation like this to yell--

FIRE!

What the--?

Nowhere to run. And mind-control is my only option.
Sorry, Astrid, but this situation is definitely--

--life--
--or--
--DEATH!
My--my mind powers!
They didn't work!

UGHH!
Let go of her, jerk!

You got 'im?
Yeah!
nnff
Get off of me!
Yeah, right. You just busted that chick's nose, loser! Somebody call campus security

FTEEN MINUTES LATER...

EMMA!

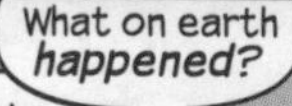
What on earth *happened?*
d date, strid. A *ally* bad date.
Max...?
Yeah.
Did he find out ou're a *mutant* or something?
Something.
Where *is* he so I can render him *incapable* of having offspring?!
They already took him away...
I'm beginning to realize more and more they're **not** *like us, Emma.*
They're **barbaric.**
Don't worry, Astrid...I'm fine. Just a bit shaken.
I know, it's just that...I just found you. I'm not ready to **lose** you.

THE NEXT DAY...

KNOCK KNOCK

Ian...?

Hi, Emma. Mind if I come in?

Suit yourself. *Christie's* not here.

I...I didn't come here to see Christie I came to see *you.* heard what happene last night and wante to make sure you were okay.

Yup. I'm as right as... *rain.*

Are...are you *sure...?* You don't sound--

Ian, I *need* you to tell me...

...is something going on between you and Christie?

ISSUE 17

Greg Horn

EMPIRE STATE UNIVERSITY
W-what?
I asked if you and Christie are *romantically involved,* Ian.
I--I--
We've been *seeing* each other for nearly two weeks, Emma.

The truth! He told me the truth.
Oh, Ian...you trusted me enough to confide in me.
Did...did Christie tell you?
No. I...just knew.
Does it bother you?
Emma, I had no idea you still had feelings for me...
...I thought it was just a high-school crush.
It was...
...but it turned into more.

And what about you, Ian?
Do you still feel the same way about me?
Emma, I-- I never felt that way toward you. I--
Ian...you're no longer my teacher and I'm no longer your student, so please...
...just admit it.
It's...it's difficult to put into words, Emma. It was like we were on the same wavelength-- like you knew exactly what I was thinking when I was thinking it.
You were unlike any student-- any woman--I'd ever met. After a while, my heart would go into overdrive whenever you walked into my classroom.
It was wrong for me to have such feelings towards a student, Emma--towards a minor.
But I'm all grown-up now, Ian. So tell me...
...is it still wrong?

BLOOM
PART 5 of 6
BETTER DAYS

WASHINGTON SQUARE PARK
THE FOLLOWING MORNING...
You kissed him?
Yes.
And he kissed you back?
Of course he did! Ian's always had a thing for me, Astrid.
Christie was no competition, really. Ian's dating her was more than likely his subconscious way of getting my attention.
y, aren't we getting just a bit full of ourselves, darling?
Just telling it like it is.
Well, Emma, I can't say I'm displeased with this turn of events.
After everything you and Ian have been through, I'm glad to see that you're finally together.

Besides which, now I won't have to listen to you speaking incessantly about him and "that traitorous skank."
That's because I'll be speaking incessantly about him and me!
Suit yourself, luv. I'm just glad you're in better spirits...
...especially after what happened on your date with Max the other night.
What happened to him, Astrid?
Last I heard he'd been kicked out of university, and rightly so, after the way he attacked you.
Good riddance, mate.
I meant, what happened to his personality? He seemed like such a nice guy. Why did he become so angry because I wanted to take our relationship slower?

When I tried to take control of his *mind*... I *couldn't.*
I pushed my mutant abilities to the *limit,* but still nothing. If those other students hadn't come along...

Don't fret, darling. It's no big deal. You're still new at it, and besides...

...I'll bet you were too freaked-out to properly concentrate. God knows I would be--
Hey.

What?

You think I'm really getting too *full* of myself?

Take it as a compliment, darling. Now, come on...
...or we'll be late for class!

E.S.U.-LATER...

Hi, Christie...

Hey...
...you backstabbing tramp.

She knows about Ian and me.
She *knows.*

Christie... what's *wrong?*
Don't feign *ignorance,* Emma.

Ian told me *everything.*

How could you *do* this to me?

Do *what?*

Steal my *boyfriend,* Emma--*that's* what!

You and Ian were *dating?* Funny how *this* is the first time I'm hearing about it from you.

When I asked what was new with you the other day, you forgot to mention that part!
It was none of your business!
And this is none of yours.
I can't share a room with you anymore.
So what are we going to do about it?

'ello! ello! 'ello, roomie!
Hope you're not a neat freak!
Neat?
Hardly.
Got to hand it to you, luv...

...it was a master stroke having me switch rooms with Christie.
I just figured everyone would be happier this way. I really appreciate you doing this, Astrid.
Think nothing of it!
Now, we're more than just mutants, Emma...we're like sisters!
I'm so glad to be rid of Christie. The entire situation was too awkward for words.
She was so resentful of Ian choosing me over her. You should have heard the things she said!

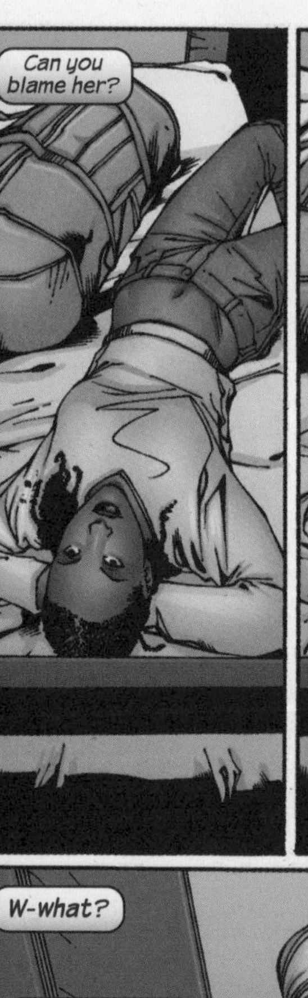
Can you blame her?

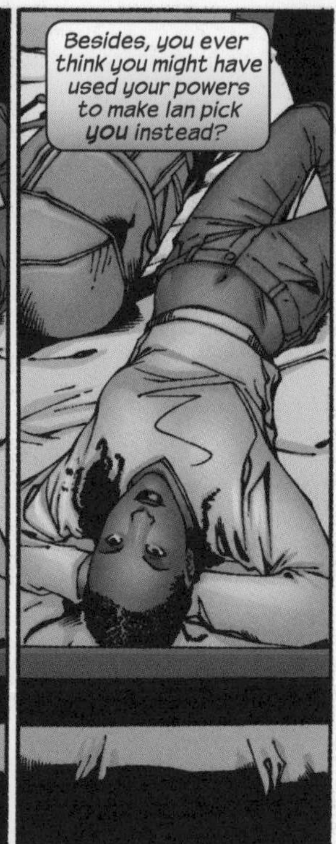
Besides, you ever think you might have used your powers to make Ian pick you instead?

W-what?
That's... that's...utterly preposterous. Ridiculous. Unthinkable.

No need to assault me with adjectives, darling. It was simply a theory.
Yes. A laughable, unfounded, highly speculative theory.

Isn't it?
It has to be.
Ian is genuinely in love with me.
JENNA HAIR DYE
Besides...
...I barely have a handle on my mind control.
Right?

CENTRAL PARK—A WEEK LATER...
So why did you decide to break up with her, Ian?
Well I, uh... I really couldn't see myself dating you and Christie, Emma.
I know, I know, but did you feel like it was a...
..conscious decision?
No...I was brainwashed by the space aliens!
But c'mon, Emma, why all the strange--?
You know...

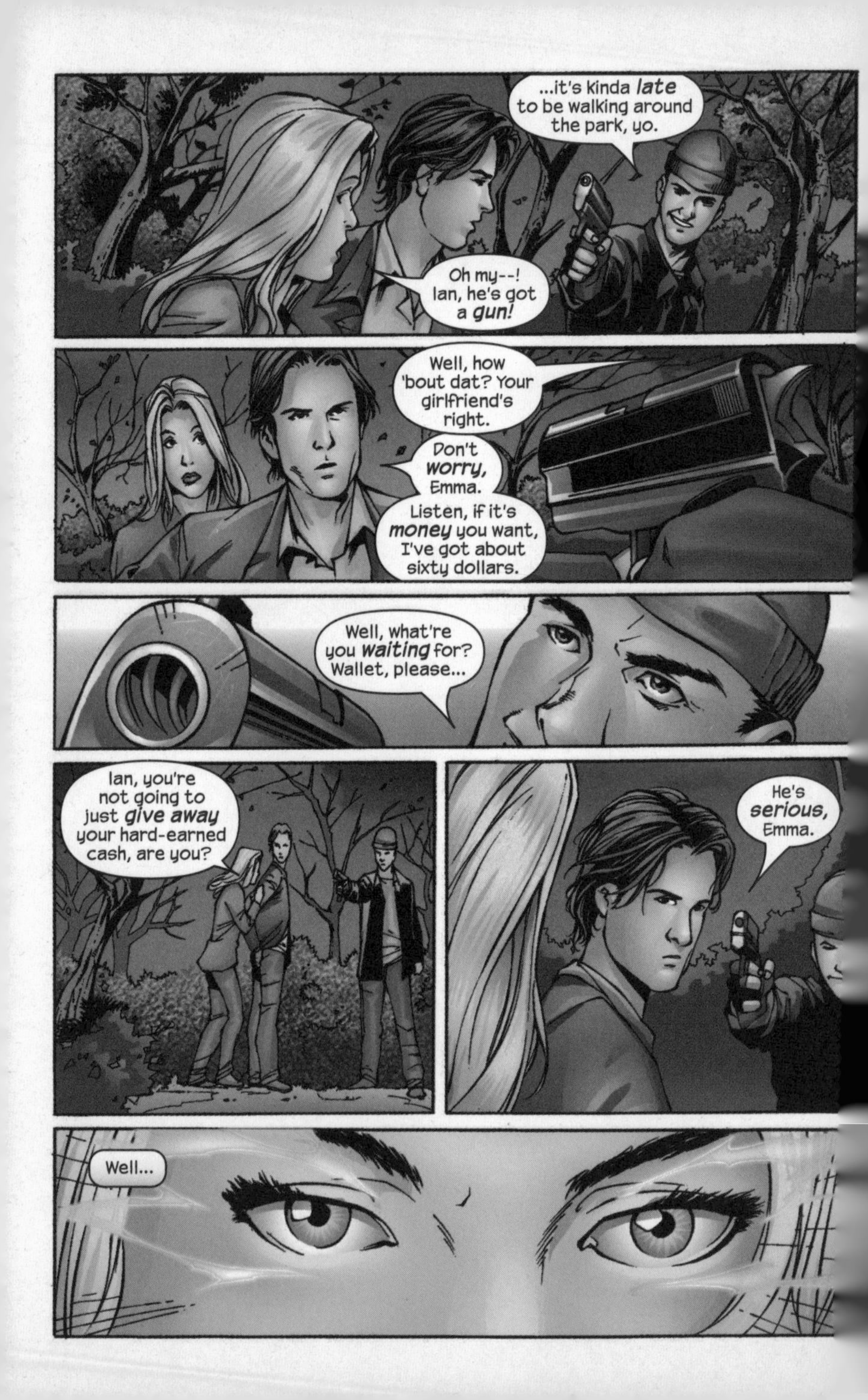
...it's kinda late to be walking around the park, yo.
Oh my--! Ian, he's got a gun!
Well, how 'bout dat? Your girlfriend's right.
Don't worry, Emma.
Listen, if it's money you want, I've got about sixty dollars.
Well, what're you waiting for? Wallet, please...
Ian, you're not going to just give away your hard-earned cash, are you?
He's serious, Emma.
Well...

...so am I!
Here. Take it. It's all I--
Uh-uh. That won't be necessary.
And here, keep an eye on this for me, okay?
What the--?
I can't watch this!
Ha, ha, ha, ha!
Ha, ha, ha, ha!
'Bye now!

Emma, was that entirely odd or did I miss something altogether?
Yes.

BRRRT BRRRT

McDermott, Christie 917-555-4380
It's *Christie.*

Hi. O-of course.
I'll be there in a half hour.

Ian, where are you going?
Sorry, Emma... but she says it's really important and can't *wait.*

I'll see you back at *campus.*
Yeah...

...see you.

Hey, Christie. What's up?
Hello, Ian.
What is it? You made it sound as if--
You broke my heart, Ian...
Christie, we only dated for like, two weeks--
So that makes it not hurt?
Listen, I--I'm sorry...
No, I don't think you are...

...but after I report you and Emma to the office of the school administrator, I'll be way more convinced!
Christie, please. Don't do this.
I won't. If you break up with Emma...
...I swear I won't.
You're such a hypocrite!
Do you think losing my job will prevent me from being with her?
Think it over, Ian. You have until tomorrow.
I've thought it over, luv...
What are you--

...and *this* is my decision.
glk

What's *wrong*, darling? Can't live with it?

UNH!
kaff koff gasp

Christie...? Christie! Oh my--! I'm so *sorry!* I-- I don't know *what* came over me!

Yeah right, *psycho!*
I'm *definitely* going to mention this *"incident"* when I speak to the *administrator!*

Christie-- *wait!*

CHRISTIE!
Perfect.
Everything's going according to plan...

ISSUE 18

Hi, Ian!
What? That's crazy! Why? How?
Shhhh!
EMPIRE STATE UNIVERSITY LIBRARY
Ian? Hold on just a minute.

Um... listen, Leila--
How do you know my na--?

Please. Don't interrupt.
I know you resent the fact that I'm young and I've got my entire life ahead of me...

...but, honestly, it's not my fault you weren't able to jumpstart that acting career all those years back.
I--
So instead of venting your frustrations daily on the E.S.U. student body...

...why don't you flex that cellulite and go on some auditions...
...or just be a dear and head back to the card catalog?

LIBRAR
Ian?
You were saying...?

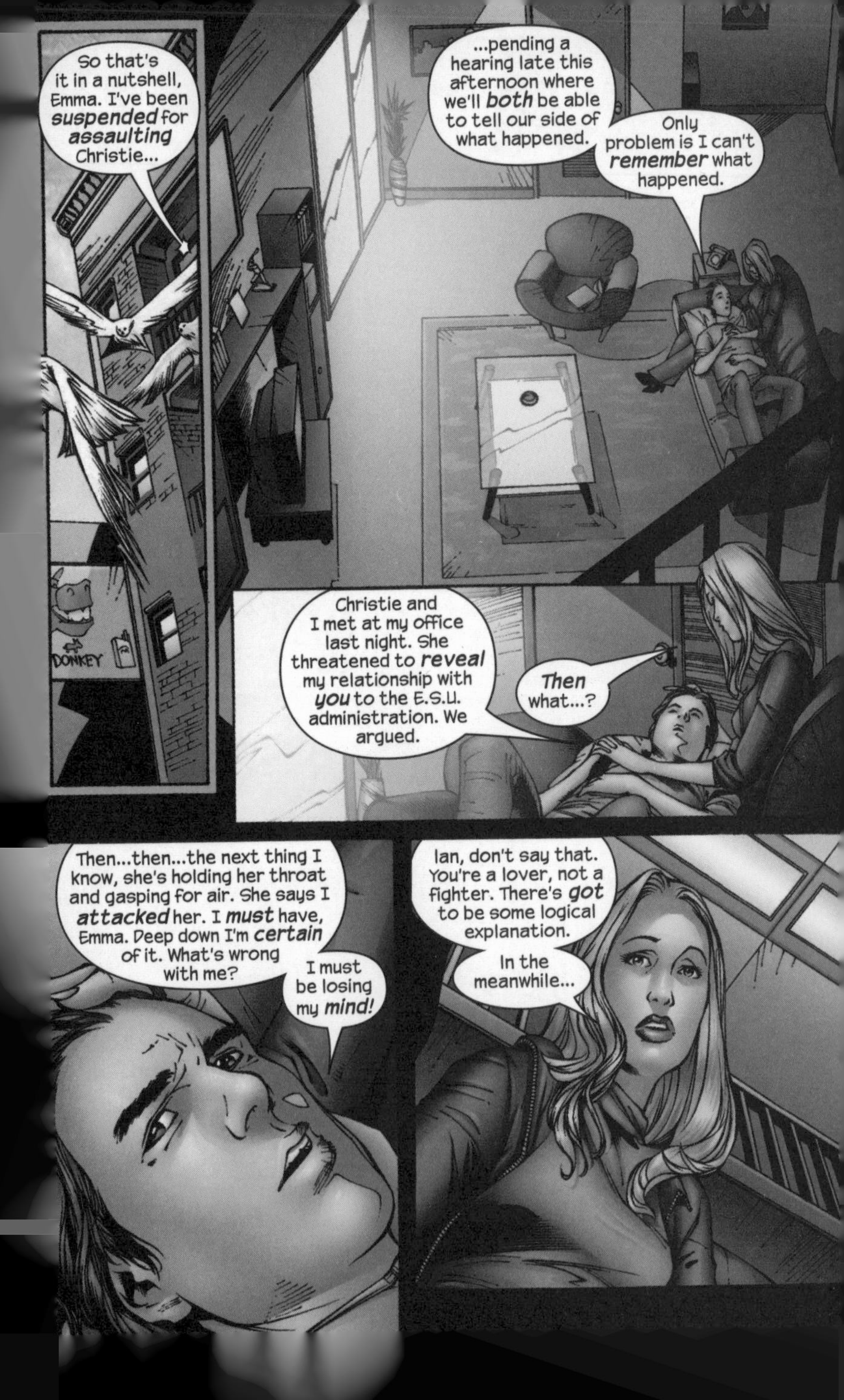
So that's it in a nutshell, Emma. I've been *suspended* for *assaulting* Christie...
...pending a hearing late this afternoon where we'll *both* be able to tell our side of what happened.
Only problem is I can't *remember* what happened.
DONKEY
Christie and I met at my office last night. She threatened to *reveal* my relationship with *you* to the E.S.U. administration. We argued.
Then what...?
Then...then...the next thing I know, she's holding her throat and gasping for air. She says I *attacked* her. I *must* have, Emma. Deep down I'm *certain* of it. What's wrong with me?
I must be losing my *mind!*
Ian, don't say that. You're a lover, not a fighter. There's *got* to be some logical explanation.
In the meanwhile...

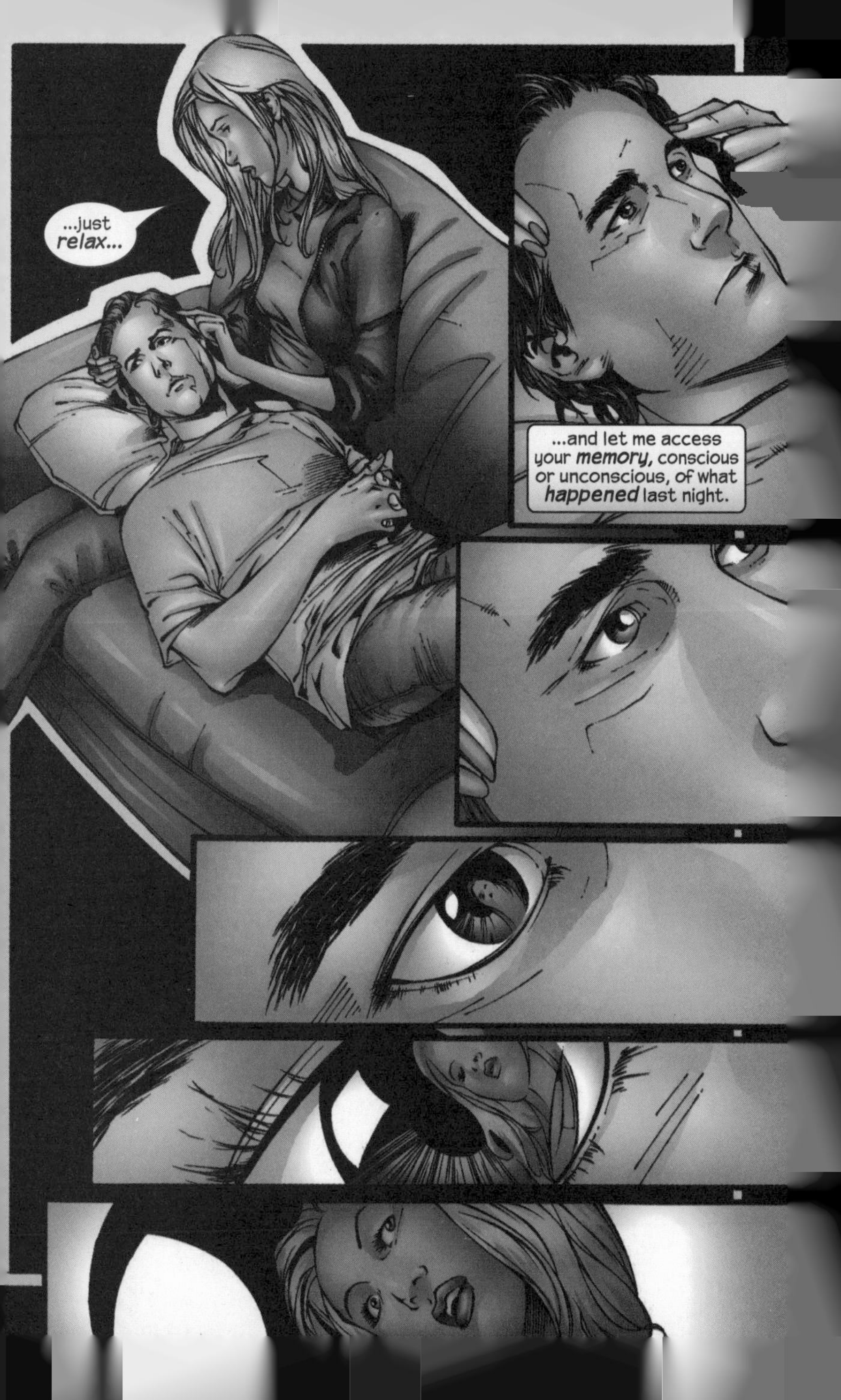
...just relax...
...and let me access your memory, conscious or unconscious, of what happened last night.

Wow. It worked.
Astrid was right.
Christie, please. Don't do this.
I won't. If you break up with Emma...I swear I won't.
...but after I report you and Emma to the office of the school administrator, I'll be way more convinced!
You're such a hypocrite!
Do you think losing my job will prevent me from being with her?
Think it over, Ian. You have until tomorrow.
What the--?
A blank spot? A gap in his memory?
kaff
koff
gasp
That didn't make sense. I should've been able to see the memory even if it was repressed.
Time to dig deeper.

AMPUS--NOON
Christie!
Emma. What do you want?
You'd better not be trying to change my minc about what happened with Ian last night.
No...
...just probing it to piece together a puzzle.
I've thought it over, luv, and this is my decision.
glk
What's wrong, darling? Can't live with it?
Oh, no.
What?
No!
What?
He did it!

LATER

A blank spot?
Gaping, Astrid.
Funny occurrence, that.
Tell me about it. Yet, I saw Ian's attack in Christie's mind.
But why doesn't he remember the assault? If anyone should've been traumatized into forgetting, it should be Christie.

Hm. You got me, luv. It doesn't make much in t
way of logical sense...

No, not unless he'd been mind-controlled by a telepath...
...isn't that right?

Emma. Dear. I know how this all looks, but if you just allow me a chance to explain, it'll be clear to you that I was simply an agent acting in your own best interest.
Remember how you saw things differently once I brought you into bloom? Remember? You're still in bloom, you know. Here. Take my ha--
Don't you touch me!

Ian is my boyfriend, Astrid! How could you do this?!
I thought you were my friend!
I am your friend, Emma! More than a friend. I'm not all bad. Ian's just going to hurt you in the end, anyway.
I've stopped him. Now, he can't hurt you. I did this for you, luv.
Stop callin me that--
--and get out of my head!
Oh, no. Max. You did it to Max, too...
For you.
...made him lose his scholarship...
All for you.
Liar! You said it was wrong to use our gifts to control other human beings!

So, I manipulated their minds to my own advantage. Was it good? Was it evil? Save the debating for philosophy class, Emma.
Life isn't black-and-white. You'll see that someday.
Astrid, you have to help me fix this. Ian needs our help. We have to make things right again.
No.
It's beneath me.
I groom you and he's the one who benefits?
Do you think he understands you? Wise up. He never will. Not like I do.
I don't have the time for this. Ian's hearing starts in half an hour and if you're not going to do anything to help, then I will!
I don't think so.
Astrid, let go of--

--me.
What *is* this, Astrid?!
Where am I?!
In a safe place, luv...

Oh, this? I've pulled you into my psyche for the duration.
What? You didn't think I'd teach you all my tricks, did you?
...where you can sit it out while that dreary it Christie does her part to get your fancy man sacked.
Trust me--this is for your own good. Look at you, poor thing, so caught up in the petty affairs of these...these bugs.
They're not like us.
What have you done to me?!
They're soulless meat puppets, Emma.
Ours to do with as we please.
Even if that means cutting their strings.
You...your parents...they... they didn't kick you out. Y-you mind-controlled your sister, Yvonne, and made her...made her...
Astrid, s-she was only...only five years old.

Now, she's eleven--
--and quite daft from what the doctors at the institution say. Such is life.
But let's try to stay in the moment, darling. The "real you" can take a time-out inside my noodle...
...ensuring that your more fleshy bits don't leave the building.
Don't worry. I won't keep you stuck inside the old brain-box for too long...

enough for Mister Ian Kendall to get what's *due* him. You know, I never realized that his initials are I.K.
Ick! Get it? Ha! Ha! Ha--
E-E-Emma...?
What have you...?
Astrid...
...stop.

Don't struggle, Astrid.
You can't win. Not against *me.*
Y- you're t-to *powerfu*
Of *course,* "darling."
I'm a *Frost.*

Holding me captive inside her mind was the worst possible move Astrid could have made.
While she went off on her little rant, I took an express tour of her psyche. Witnessed her complete training.
Learned everything she knew. That's how I beat her.
I thought she was my friend...but she was sick.
I'll deal with her later. Right now, I've got to clean up her mess.
But how?
"They're soulless meat puppets, Emma."

"Ours to do with as we please."
I really don't know what happened between you and that student, Kendall, but by the time she's finished in there...
SLAM
...I will. Whether I want to or not.
And I pray we're not facing a scandal, or worse-- a lawsuit-- because of it.
Okay, Christie...if you'd just begin at the... well, at the beginning...
Just take it slowly, and in your own words, tell us what occurred last night in Mister Kendall's office.
It wasn't love at first sight, y'know. It's like when you bite into a jalapeño pepper, but you don't taste anything at first.
Then, after about ten seconds, you start to feel a tingling sensation igniting your taste buds. After twenty seconds, your mouth is a raging inferno.
Uhh...Ms. McDermott, if you'd just stick to the incident in--
That's how it was with Ian.
I'm telling you...

...he was my jalapeño.
Sophisticated, talented, charming, funny and hot. Oh, Ian. Every time I saw him, the feelings inside me grew more and more intense.
And he didn't have any idea how I felt. For weeks I secretly followed him, working up the nerve, and last night...
...last night, I told him everything I just told you...a-and do you want to know what happened?
Do you want to know what he said?!
Huh?!
Well?!
Do you?!
He said he "didn't feel that way about me!" Pretty darned rude, if you ask me.
I mean, didn't he hear a word I said?!
I love him!! He's my soul mate! Doesn't he care?! Doesn't anybody?!
Christie! What on--?!
Dear Lord! Grab her arms before she hurts herself!
Let go of me! Get off!!
Basket case...

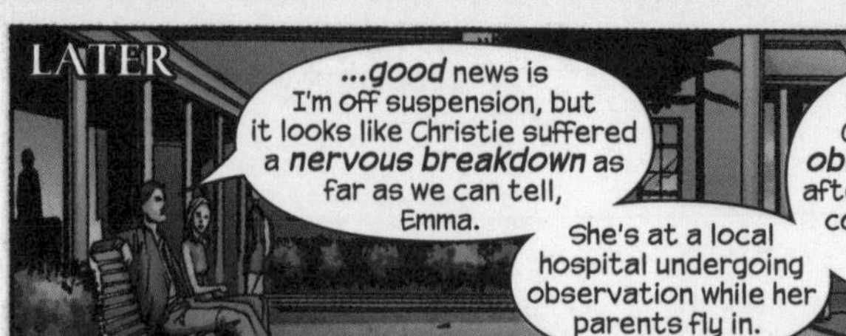

LATER
...good news is I'm off suspension, but it looks like Christie suffered a nervous breakdown as far as we can tell, Emma.
She's at a local hospital undergoing observation while her parents fly in.
The E.S.U. president thinks Christie became so obsessed with me that after I rejected her, she couldn't handle it and invented the story.

Poor kid. I never realized she had such deep emotional problems.
It...it just doesn't seem like her to do something like that.

She...she didn't.
Emma...?
It's true. You did assault her, but I...I made sure she couldn't tell the school's administrators about it.

What?
Even if any of this was true (which it isn't because it's so preposterous), how on earth could you stop her?
Because... I'm a mutant, Ian.
I took control of her mind and forced her to say those things in the conference room.

Took control of her...? Oh, come on, Emma, be serious for a minute. What on earth are you talking about?

I tell him the truth.
Every last bit until no more is left to tell.
Dear Lord. You're not joking.
Ian, wait!
Stay away from me, you-- you--
--mutie.
No wonder your grades were so perfect! You've been giving yourself an unfair advantage all this time.
It's true what the media says about you people.
Ordinary humans like me... Christie...that poor kid, Max...to you and this Astrid person, we're just playthings. Toys.
Ian!
No!
Ian. Wait. Please. You don't understand. I didn't have a choice. I never asked for these abilities. When they came, I didn't know who I could trust.
Goodbye, Emma...
B-but, Ian...
...I love you.

Roommate says she found her like this.
Heart rate, pulse, breathing... all there...
...but she's checked out.
It didn't have to end this way, Astrid. You were even responsible for my powers going out of control when I first arrived at E.S.U....
...just so I'd lose confidence and turn to you for help more readily once we'd met.
911
Were you so desperate for companionship you risked losing it just so you could hold onto it?
...looks so cold, unaffected...
...ain't she in my English Lit class...?
...think her name is Emily First or something...
QC DUDE
...bet anything she poisoned her roommate...
...wonder if campus security questioned her...?

Who cares what you think?
After all is said and done, I think Astrid was right about the whole lot of you.
The whole lot.
THE END